EGYPT

Tom Streissguth

⌐ **Lerner Publications Company • Minneapolis**

Lerner Publications Company
A division of Lerner Publishing Group, Inc.
241 First Avenue North
Minneapolis, MN 55401 U.S.A.

Website address: www.lernerbooks.com

Library of Congress Cataloging-in-Publication Data

Streissguth, Thomas, 1958–
    Egypt / by Tom Streissguth.
        p.   cm. — (Country explorers)
    Includes index.
    ISBN 978–0–8225–8660–9 (lib. bdg. : alk. paper)
    1. Egypt—Juvenile literature. I. Title.
DT49.S87 2008
962—dc22   2007021481

Manufactured in the United States of America
1 2 3 4 5 6 – PA – 13 12 11 10 09 08

Table of Contents

Egypt

ALGERIA

Welcome!

We're heading to Egypt! Egypt lies on the continent of Africa. The Nile River runs through Egypt. The Nile is the longest river in the world.

Egypt touches the countries of Sudan in the south and Libya in the west. The Red Sea sits to the east. The Mediterranean Sea is north of Egypt. The Sinai Peninsula attaches Egypt to the continent of Asia.

LIBYA

Tourists often visit Egyptian beaches on the Red Sea.

NIGER

4

CHAD

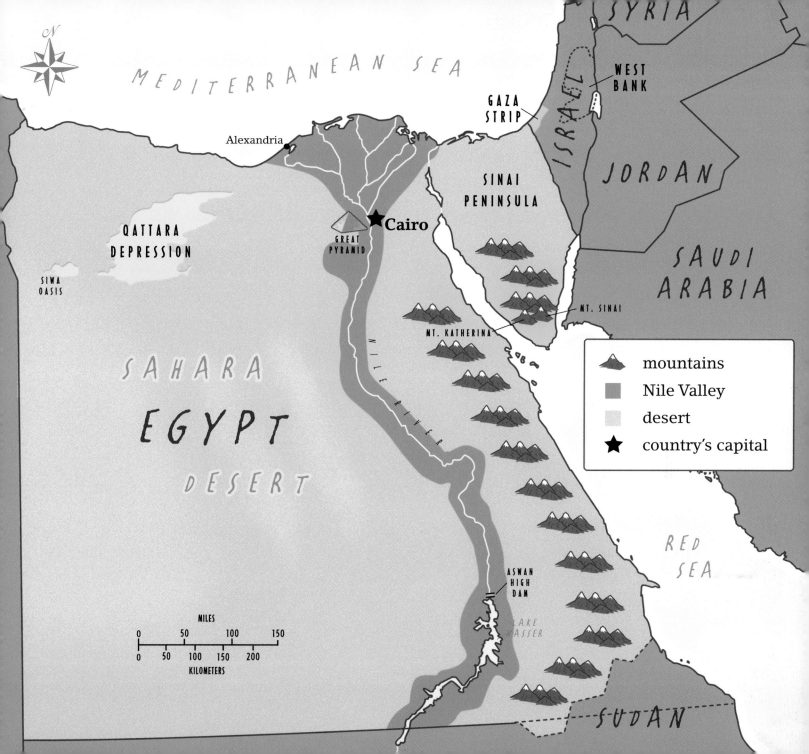

The Nile River

Would you like to sail down the Nile? Then jump on board a felucca! A felucca is an Egyptian sailboat. On a felucca, you can travel from southern Egypt to the Mediterranean Sea.

Feluccas sail on the Nile as it flows through the city of Aswan.

Toward the end of the trip, you will pass through Cairo. North of Cairo, the Nile branches into smaller rivers. They flow into the Mediterranean. The rivers form a triangle. This area is called a delta.

EGYPT

The Nile Delta seen from space

Dear Nan,
Yesterday I sailed in a felucca on the Nile! It was a windy day, so the sailboat went pretty fast. I saw lots of green fields on the riverbanks. Just past them, high red cliffs showed where the desert starts. Cool!
See you soon,

Marcy

Na

Your

Anywhe

Controlling the Nile

The Nile used to flood the riverbanks every single year. Farmers couldn't grow anything on low farmland while it was flooded.

Flooded land near the Nile, around 1950

In 1971, the Aswan High Dam was completed. It holds back water from the Nile. It keeps the river from flooding. This lets farmers grow more crops on their land.

The Aswan
High Dam

The Sahara

Egyptians do not need raincoats to keep dry! That is because the Sahara covers most of the country. The Sahara is a huge desert. Rain hardly ever falls there. Sandy fields stretch across much of the Sahara. Some parts of the desert have mountains.

Desert winds form sand dunes in many parts of the Sahara.

Not many people live in the desert. But some folks settle on oases. Oases are places in the desert where there is water. Crops and trees can grow there.

Thousands of people live at the Siwa Oasis.

Country Life

Many Egyptians live on small farms near the Nile. Egyptian farmers are called fellahin. Some fellahin raise cotton, rice, and wheat. Others grow vegetables such as corn.

Donkeys help farmers by carrying heavy loads.

Map Whiz Quiz

Trace the outline of Egypt on pages 4 and 5 onto a sheet of paper. Find the body of water to the right of Egypt. That is the Red Sea. Color it red. Mark it with an *E* for east. Find the Mediterranean Sea. Color it blue. Mark it with an *N* for north. Find the Nile River. Color it green, since green plants can grow near it.

Fellahin also tend date palm trees. Those trees supply dates, a kind of fruit.

13

Egyptians

African people have lived in Egypt for thousands of years. More than one thousand years ago, Arab people settled in Egypt too. Most modern Egyptians have both African and Arab people in their family tree.

Egyptians may have different skin color and hair, depending on their family trees.

People called Nubians used to live along the Nile in southern Egypt. Many Nubians moved to northern cities. Other Egyptians are desert nomads. Nomads travel from place to place instead of living in one spot.

Nomads

Some Egyptians are nomads. They travel across the Sahara for most of the year. One group of nomads is the Bedouin. They live in tents and herd sheep, goats, and camels. Some modern Bedouin have become farmers. The government provides schools and medical care for Bedouin farmers.

A Bedouin couple

This Egyptian family takes a ride on camels.

Family

How many brothers and sisters do you have? In Egypt, parents like to have big families. Most kids have three, four, or five brothers and sisters.

Egyptian families stick together. Many married couples live with the husband's parents. The husband's brothers, their families, and his sisters might squeeze in too. The house can get really crowded! But Egyptians don't mind. They love to have their families nearby.

A large family visits the pyramids.

Big City

Cairo is the largest city in Egypt. It's also the country's capital. Cairo has modern skyscrapers, freeways, and colorful signs. But it also has traditional shops and cafés.

The Nile River flows by downtown Cairo.

Cairo is one of the most crowded cities in the world! Many Egyptians have moved there to find jobs. About sixteen million people live in Cairo. How many people live in your city?

Cairo's busy streets can be very loud and jammed with traffic.

Cairo's streets are very busy. Cars pass people riding donkeys. Horses pull carts past kids playing soccer. Some people push carts loaded with goods to sell. The carts are like stores on wheels.

19

Homes

Some people live above shops in Egypt's cities. Others live in tall apartment buildings. In the country, Egyptians build houses from mud bricks. Most houses have two rooms. People gather and eat in one room. They sleep in the other.

A traditional mud-brick house

Some Egyptian houses have a courtyard in the middle. People might cook their meals in courtyards. People also keep their animals in their courtyard at night. Animals stay safe there.

Some houses are painted with brightly colored murals.

Arabic

Egyptians speak Arabic. Egyptian kids learn how to read and write Arabic in school. People write and read Arabic from right to left.

Picture Writing

In ancient times, Egyptians used pictures to write. These pictures are called hieroglyphs (HY-roh-glihfs). The symbols decorate the walls of tombs and other ancient buildings.

Religion

Most Egyptians are Muslims. Muslims follow the religion of Islam. They often go to pray at mosques. A mosque is an Islamic house of prayer. Egypt's cities and villages have many mosques.

Inside the Al-Azhar Mosque, Cairo's oldest mosque

Most mosques have a minaret. A minaret is a tall, thin tower. A man called a muezzin climbs the minaret five times a day. He calls out a chant from the top. The chant reminds Muslims that it is time to pray.

This mosque and minaret are in the city of Alexandria on the Mediterranean Sea.

Festivals!

Egyptians celebrate springtime on a holiday called *Sham al-Nessim*. That means "scent of the breeze." On this holiday, Egyptian families enjoy picnics at gardens or at parks.

In Cairo, Egyptians swim and row boats on the Nile on Sham al-Nessim.

Ramadan

Ramadan is the holy month of the Islamic calendar. Muslims fast during the days of Ramadan. They don't eat or drink anything from sunrise until sunset. They eat a meal called *iftar* at sundown, and friends and families often eat together. Many people follow the rules of Islam more closely during Ramadan.

At the end of Ramadan, Egyptians celebrate Eid al-Fitr. They gather with family and have a large feast.

Mawlid al-Nabi marks the birthday of Muhammad. Muhammad started Islam. On Mawlid al-Nabi, big tents fill the streets. Egyptians bang drums and shake tambourines inside the tents. Some people dance and sing. At night, a parade winds through the town.

Muslims share the iftar meal at sundown during Ramadan.

27

Learning

At the age of six, Egyptian kids start
elementary school. Around the age of twelve,
they begin middle school. Lots of children go
to work after they are fourteen years old.
Others move on to high school and college.

Egyptian schools are crowded! Egyptian students often have to share their books, desks, and seats. The government has built many new schools to help change this.

Girls share desks at a school in Cairo. Many Egyptian schools have separate classrooms for girls and boys.

Shopping

Shoppers in most Egyptian towns go to the souk. A souk is a marketplace. People buy and sell many types of goods there. One lane of the souk is lined with rug stores. Another area offers copper pans. Spices are for sale nearby.

Egyptians shop at an outdoor market in Cairo.

There are no price tags at a souk. A buyer and a seller bargain over the price of an item. They try to find a price they agree on.

Camel Buying

If you plan to cross the Sahara, head to the camel market in Cairo! Camels are very useful animals to the Egyptians. Can you guess why? Camels hardly ever need a drink of water. They can cross the desert carrying a heavy load or a rider. In cities, camels also help Egyptian families make money. Tourists often pay an Egyptian man to take them for a ride on his camel.

Clothes

Many Egyptians like to wear loose, traditional outfits to keep cool. Men often wear long, loose shirts. They wear small cloth hats called skullcaps to protect their heads from the sun. Women wear long dresses and veils.

Men may wear skullcaps (*above*) or turbans (*right*) on their heads.

Some Egyptians wear American or European clothes.
Businesspeople wear suits or dresses to work. And young
people often wear a mix of traditional and modern clothing.

Hosni Mubarak, the
president of Egypt, and
his wife, Suzanne, wear
business-style clothing.

Lunch Break

Lunch is the biggest meal of the day in Egypt. Cooks grill chunks of lamb with tomatoes, onions, peppers, and spices. Egyptians often cook with tahini. Tahini is a paste of ground sesame seeds. Baba ghanoush is a mixture of tahini and eggplant. People eat it with pita bread.

This Egyptian meal includes sweet potato salad; baba ghanoush; a salad of tomato, cucumber, and parsley with lemon juice; pita bread; and fried fish with tomatoes.

Egyptians like to end lunch with fruit. Still hungry? Egyptians love to snack on sweet, sticky treats made with honey.

Pita bread is cooked in big clay ovens.

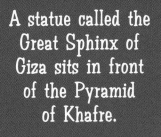

A statue called the Great Sphinx of Giza sits in front of the Pyramid of Khafre.

The Pyramids

In ancient times, kings called pharaohs ruled Egypt. Pharaohs had workers build giant, pyramid-shaped buildings of stone. A king would be buried inside when he died.

Thousands of years ago, a pharaoh named Khufu had workers build the Great Pyramid. When Khufu died, valuable treasures were placed in the pyramid with his body. Visitors can see the empty room where the goods once were.

The Great Pyramid *(front)* and other pyramids are in Giza, a city near Cairo.

School's Out!

Egyptian kids love to play soccer. After school, they play in the streets or on school teams. They also like *seega*. Seega is a little bit like tic-tac-toe.

Boys play soccer at the Siwa Oasis.

Egyptian kids help their families too. Many do after-school chores on farms or babysit their younger brothers and sisters. Other kids help their parents catch fish or sell goods in markets.

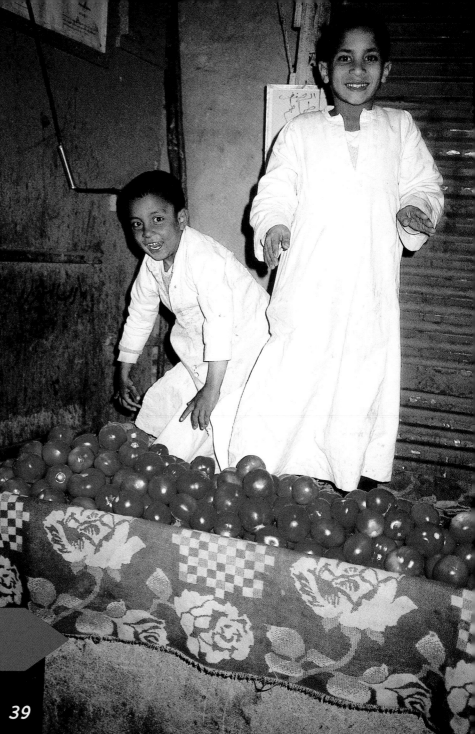

These children are selling tomatoes.

Shows to Watch

Lights! Camera! Action! More movies are made in Egypt than in any other country in Africa. Action, romance, and comedy films are popular.

People wait near a poster for an Egyptian movie in 2004.

40

Egypt produces TV shows too. Egyptian game shows, sitcoms, and dramas are shown in other Arab countries.

First Ladies Laura Bush (*left*) and Suzanne Mubarak visit the set of the Egyptian *Sesame Street*.

Music

Egyptians like lots of different types of music. Farmers and boaters on the Nile sing folk songs. Street musicians might play the flute or the *rebab*. The rebab is like a violin.

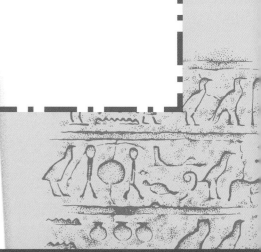

The Egyptian band Wust el Balad plays a mix of jazz, blues, Latin, and Arabic music.

Egyptian dance music is popular in Egypt and nearby countries. But some Egyptians prefer American rock music or European opera tunes.

Hakim, one of Egypt's biggest pop stars

43

THE FLAG OF EGYPT

Egypt's flag has a red stripe on top, a white stripe in the middle, and a black stripe at the bottom. The red stands for Egypt's struggle for independence. The white stands for the Egyptian Revolution of 1952, when Egyptians took over their government. They put a president in charge instead of a king. The black stripe stands for the end of hard times the Egyptians suffered under kings and queens. A golden eagle sits in the center of the flag. The eagle's feet hold a scroll with the country's name written in Arabic.

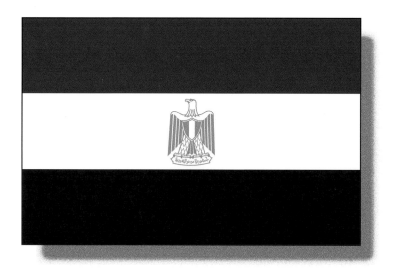

FAST FACTS

FULL COUNTRY NAME: Arab Republic of Egypt

AREA: 386,660 square miles (1,001,450 square kilometers), or about the size of the states of Texas and California combined

MAIN LANDFORMS: the Sinai Peninsula, the mountains Sinai and Katherina, the Sahara desert, the desert basin called Qattara Depression

MAJOR RIVERS: Nile River

ANIMALS AND THEIR HABITATS: camels (desert), crocodiles (Nile), cobras (desert, villages), flamingos (along Nile), golden eagles (near Nile), horned vipers (desert), hyenas (mountains, grasslands), scorpions (desert), tiger sharks (ocean)

CAPITAL CITY: Cairo

OFFICIAL LANGUAGE: Arabic

POPULATION: about 80,335,036

GLOSSARY

continent: any one of seven large areas of land. The continents are Africa, Antarctica, Asia, Australia, Europe, North America, and South America.

courtyard: an open area surrounded by walls

delta: a triangle-shaped area of land where a river enters the sea. The river leaves behind mud or sand on the delta.

desert: a dry, sandy region

desert basin: a sunken area of a desert

hieroglyphs: pictures and symbols that ancient Egyptians used in writing

mummies: dead bodies that ancient Egyptians wrapped in cloth to save them for a long time

Muslim: a person who practices the religion of Islam

nomad: a person who wanders from place to place instead of living in one spot

oases: places in the desert where there is water. Trees and crops can grow on an oasis.

peninsula: an area of land with water on three sides

pharaohs: kings of ancient Egypt

pyramid: a stone building with four triangle-shaped sides, built by ancient Egyptians

TO LEARN MORE

BOOKS

Haskins, Jim, and Kathleen Benson. *Count Your Way through Egypt.* Minneapolis: Millbrook Press, 2007. Learn to count from one to ten in Arabic as you find out more about Egypt.

Husain, Shahrukh. *Egypt.* North Mankato, MN: Smart Apple Media, 2005. This is a collection of stories from ancient Egypt.

Meister, Cari. *Nile River.* Edina, MN: Abdo Publishing, 2002. Learn where the world's longest river starts, what animals call it home, and how it helps Egyptians and other Africans.

WEBSITES

Ancient Egypt
http://www.ancientegypt.co.uk/menu .html
This interactive website by the British Museum lets you explore ancient Egypt, including daily life, pharaohs, mummies, and writing. It features stories, lots of photos, and challenges.

Time for Kids—Egypt
http://www.timeforkids.com/TFK/hh/ goplaces/main/0,20344,535892,00.html
Visit this website to learn simple phrases in Arabic or spend a day in the life of a twelve-year-old Egyptian. You can also view a timeline of Egypt's history and send an electronic postcard.

INDEX

The photographs in this book are used with the permission of: © Gerard Hancock/Art Directors, p. 4; © Michele Burgess, pp. 6, 16, 18; NASA, p. 7; © Paul Almasy/CORBIS, p. 8; © Jon Arnold Images/Alamy, p. 9; © age fotostock/SuperStock, pp. 10, 21, 24, 31, 34; © Kurt Scholz/SuperStock, p. 11; AP Photo/Ben Curtis, p. 12; © Kevin Fleming/CORBIS, p. 13; © Cory Langley, pp. 14, 20; © SuperStock, Inc./SuperStock, p. 15; © Nik Wheeler/CORBIS, p. 17; © P L Mitchell/Art Directors, p. 19; © saturno dona'/Alamy, p. 22; © Gregor Schuster/zefa/Corbis, p. 23; © Bettmann/CORBIS, p. 25; AP Photo/Amr Nabil, p. 26; © Khaled Desouki/AFP/Getty Images, p. 27; © Jean Dominique DALLET/Alamy, p. 28; AP Photo/Mohamed El-Dakhakhny, p. 29; © David Harding/Art Directors, p. 30; © Thomas Hartwell/CORBIS, p. 32 (left); © Adina Tovy/Art Directors, p. 32 (right); AP Photo/Jalil Bounhar, p. 33; © Michele Burgess/SuperStock, p. 35; © David Sutherland/Photographer's Choice/Getty Images, p. 36; © Scott Olson/Getty Images, p. 37 (left); © Martin Gray/National Geographic/Getty Images, p. 37 (right); © Sylvain Grandadam/The Image Bank/Getty Images, p. 38; © John R. Kreul/Independent Picture Service, p. 39; AP Photo/Talal Amr, p. 40; © AFP/Getty Images, p. 41; AP Photo/Mohamed al Sehety, p. 42; AP Photo/John McConnico, p. 43. Illustrations by © Bill Hauser/Independent Picture Service.

Cover: © Jose Fuste Raga/CORBIS